Welcome to Good Morning Girls! We are so glad you are joining us.

God created us to walk with Him, to know Him, and to be loved by Him. He is our living well, and when we drink from the water He continually provides, His living water will change the entire course of our lives.

Jesus said: "Whoever drinks of the water that I will give him will never be thirsty again. The water that I will give him will become in him a spring of water welling up to eternal life." ~John 4:14 (ESV)

So let's begin.

The method we use here at GMG is called the SOAK method.

☐ **S**—The S stands for **Scripture.** Read the chapter for the day. Then choose 1-2 verses and write them out word for word. (There is no right or wrong choice—just let the Holy Spirit guide you.)

☐ **O**—The O stands for **Observation.** Look at the verse or verses you wrote out. Write 1 or 2 observations. What stands out to you? What do you learn about the character of God from these verses? Is there a promise, command or teaching?

☐ **A**—The A stands for **Application.** Personalize the verses. What is God saying to you? How can you apply them to your life? Are there any changes you need to make or an action to take?

☐ **K**—The K stands for **Kneeling in Prayer.** Pause, kneel and pray. Confess any sin God has revealed to you today. Praise God for His word. Pray the passage over your own life or someone you love. Ask God to help you live out your applications.

SOAK God's word into your heart and squeeze every bit of nourishment you can out of each day's scripture reading. Soon you will find your life transformed by the renewing of your mind!

Walk with the King!

Courtney

WomenLivingWell.org, GoodMorningGirls.org

Join the GMG Community

Share your daily SOAK at 7:45am on
Facebook.com/GoodMorningGirlsWLW
Instagram.com/WomenLivingWell #GoodMorningGirls

THE BOOK OF Proverbs

ONE CHAPTER A DAY

GoodMorningGirls.org

The Book of Proverbs

GMG Bible Coloring Chart

COLORS	KEYWORDS
PURPLE	God, Jesus, Holy Spirit, Saviour, Messiah
PINK	women of the Bible, family, marriage, parenting, friendship, relationships
RED	love, kindness, mercy, compassion, peace, grace
GREEN	faith, obedience, growth, fruit, salvation, fellowship, repentance
YELLOW	worship, prayer, praise, doctrine, angels, miracles, power of God, blessings
BLUE	wisdom, teaching, instruction, commands
ORANGE	prophecy, history, times, places, kings, genealogies, people, numbers, covenants, vows, visions, oaths, future
BROWN/GRAY	Satan, sin, death, hell, evil, idols, false teachers, hypocrisy, temptation

The fear of the Lord is
the beginning of knowledge;
fools despise wisdom and instruction.

Proverbs 1:7

Proverbs 1

S—The S stands for **Scripture**

O—The O stands for **Observation**

A—The A stands for **Application**

K—The K stands for **Kneeling in Prayer**

For the Lord gives wisdom;

from his mouth come knowledge

and understanding.

Proverbs 2:6

Proverbs 2

S—The S stands for *Scripture*

O—The O stands for *Observation*

A—The A stands for *Application*

K—The K stands for *Kneeling in Prayer*

Trust in the Lord with all your heart,

and do not lean on your own understanding.

In all your ways acknowledge him,

and he will make straight your paths.

Proverbs 3:5,6

Proverbs 3

S—The S stands for *Scripture*

O—The O stands for *Observation*

A—The A stands for *Application*

K—The K stands for *Kneeling in Prayer*

Keep your heart
with all vigilance,
for from it flow
the springs of life.

Proverbs 4:23

Proverbs 4

S—The S stands for *Scripture*

O—The O stands for *Observation*

A—The A stands for *Application*

K—The K stands for *Kneeling in Prayer*

For a man's ways are before

the eyes of the Lord,

and he ponders

all his paths.

Proverbs 5:21

Proverbs 5

S—The S stands for *Scripture*

O—The O stands for *Observation*

A—The A stands for *Application*

K—The K stands for *Kneeling in Prayer*

Go to the ant, O sluggard;

consider her ways

and be wise.

Proverbs 6:6

Proverbs 6

S—The S stands for **Scripture**

O—The O stands for **Observation**

A—The A stands for **Application**

K—The K stands for **Kneeling in Prayer**

Keep my commandments and live;

keep my teaching as the

apple of your eye.

Proverbs 7:2

Proverbs 7

S—The S stands for **Scripture**

O—The O stands for **Observation**

A—The A stands for **Application**

K—The K stands for **Kneeling in Prayer**

Whoever finds wisdom finds life

and obtains favor

from the Lord.

Proverbs 8:35

Proverbs 8

S—The S stands for *Scripture*

O—The O stands for *Observation*

A—The A stands for *Application*

K—The K stands for *Kneeling in Prayer*

The fear of the Lord

is the beginning of wisdom,

and the knowledge of the Holy One

is insight.

Proverbs 9:10

Proverbs 9

S – The S stands for *Scripture*

O – The O stands for *Observation*

A – The A stands for *Application*

K – The K stands for *Kneeling in Prayer*

Hatred stirs up strife,

but love covers all offenses.

Proverbs 10:12

Proverbs 10

S—The S stands for **_Scripture_**

O—The O stands for **_Observation_**

A—The A stands for **_Application_**

K—The K stands for **_Kneeling in Prayer_**

Like a gold ring
in a pig's snout
is a beautiful woman
without discretion.

Proverbs 11:22

Proverbs 11

S—The S stands for *Scripture*

O—The O stands for *Observation*

A—The A stands for *Application*

K—The K stands for *Kneeling in Prayer*

An excellent wife is the
crown of her husband,
but she who brings shame
is like rottenness
in his bones.

Proverbs 12:4

Proverbs 12

S—The S stands for *Scripture*

O—The O stands for *Observation*

A—The A stands for *Application*

K—The K stands for *Kneeling in Prayer*

Whoever walks with the wise

becomes wise,

but the companion of fools

will suffer harm.

Proverbs 13:20

Proverbs 13

S—The S stands for **Scripture**

O—The O stands for **Observation**

A—The A stands for **Application**

K—The K stands for **Kneeling in Prayer**

Whoever is slow to anger

has great understanding,

but he who has a hasty temper

exalts folly.

Proverbs 14:29

Proverbs 14

S—The S stands for *Scripture*

O—The O stands for *Observation*

A—The A stands for *Application*

K—The K stands for *Kneeling in Prayer*

A soft answer turns

away wrath

but a harsh word

stirs up anger.

Proverbs 15:1

Proverbs 15

S—The S stands for ***Scripture***

O—The O stands for ***Observation***

A—The A stands for ***Application***

K—The K stands for ***Kneeling in Prayer***

Gracious words

are like a honeycomb,

sweetness to the soul

and health to the body.

Proverbs 16:24

Proverbs 16

S—The S stands for *Scripture*

O—The O stands for *Observation*

A—The A stands for *Application*

K—The K stands for *Kneeling in Prayer*

Whoever covers an offense seeks love,

but he who repeats a matter

separates close friends.

Proverbs 17:9

Proverbs 17

S—The S stands for *Scripture*

O—The O stands for *Observation*

A—The A stands for *Application*

K—The K stands for *Kneeling in Prayer*

The name of the Lord
is a strong tower:
the righteous man runs
into it and is safe.

Proverbs 18:10

Proverbs 18

S — The S stands for **Scripture**

O — The O stands for **Observation**

A — The A stands for **Application**

K — The K stands for **Kneeling in Prayer**

Whoever is generous to the poor

lends to the Lord,

and he will repay him

for his deed.

Proverbs 19:17

Proverbs 19

S—The S stands for *Scripture*

O—The O stands for *Observation*

A—The A stands for *Application*

K—The K stands for *Kneeling in Prayer*

Wine is a mocker,

strong drink a brawler,

and whoever is led astray by it

is not wise.

Proverbs 20:1

Proverbs 20

S—The S stands for *Scripture*

O—The O stands for *Observation*

A—The A stands for *Application*

K—The K stands for *Kneeling in Prayer*

It is better to live

in a desert land

than with a quarrelsome

and fretful woman.

Proverbs 21:19

Proverbs 21

S—The S stands for *Scripture*

O—The O stands for *Observation*

A—The A stands for *Application*

K—The K stands for *Kneeling in Prayer*

Train up a child
in the way he should go;
even when he is old
he will not depart from it.

Proverbs 22:6

Proverbs 22

S—The S stands for *Scripture*

O—The O stands for *Observation*

A—The A stands for *Application*

K—The K stands for *Kneeling in Prayer*

Let not your heart envy sinners,

but continue in

the fear of the Lord

all the day.

Proverbs 23:17

Proverbs 23

S—The S stands for *Scripture*

O—The O stands for *Observation*

A—The A stands for *Application*

K—The K stands for *Kneeling in Prayer*

By wisdom a house is built,

and by understanding

it is established.

Proverbs 24:3

Proverbs 24

S—The S stands for **Scripture**

O—The O stands for **Observation**

A—The A stands for **Application**

K—The K stands for **Kneeling in Prayer**

If you enemy is hungry,

give him bread to eat,

and if he is thirsty,

give him water to drink,

for you will heap burning coals on his head,

and the Lord will reward you.

Proverbs 25:21,22

Proverbs 25

S—The S stands for *Scripture*

O—The O stands for *Observation*

A—The A stands for *Application*

K—The K stands for *Kneeling in Prayer*

Whoever meddles in a
quarrel not his own
is like one who takes
a passing dog by the ears.

Proverbs 26:17

Proverbs 26

S—The S stands for *Scripture*

O—The O stands for *Observation*

A—The A stands for *Application*

K—The K stands for *Kneeling in Prayer*

Iron sharpens iron,

and one man

sharpens another.

Proverbs 27:17

Proverbs 27

S—The S stands for *Scripture*

O—The O stands for *Observation*

A—The A stands for *Application*

K—The K stands for *Kneeling in Prayer*

Whoever conceals his transgressions

will not prosper,

but he who confesses and forsakes them

will obtain mercy.

Proverbs 28:13

Proverbs 28

S—The S stands for *Scripture*

O—The O stands for *Observation*

A—The A stands for *Application*

K—The K stands for *Kneeling in Prayer*

The fear of man

lays a snare,

but whoever trusts in the Lord

is safe.

Proverbs 29:25

Proverbs 29

S—The S stands for ***Scripture***

O—The O stands for ***Observation***

A—The A stands for ***Application***

K—The K stands for ***Kneeling in Prayer***

Every word of God

proves true;

he is a shield to those

who take refuge in him.

Proverbs 30:5

Proverbs 30

S—The S stands for **Scripture**

O—The O stands for **Observation**

A—The A stands for **Application**

K—The K stands for **Kneeling in Prayer**

Charm is deceitful,

and beauty is vain,

but a woman who

fears the Lord

is to be praised.

Proverbs 31:30

Proverbs 31

S—The S stands for **_Scripture_**

O—The O stands for **_Observation_**

A—The A stands for **_Application_**

K—The K stands for **_Kneeling in Prayer_**

Made in United States
Orlando, FL
19 July 2022